What Am I?

What Kind of BIRD AM I?

Taylor Farley

TABLE OF CONTENTS

A Crabtree Seedlings Book

What Kind of Bird Am I?

I have pink feathers and long, thin legs.

What kind of bird am I?

A flamingo

I have big, round eyes that can see at night.

What kind of bird am I?

An owl

I have both black and white feathers, but I cannot fly.

What kind of bird am I?

A penguin

I have webbed feet and catch fish in my pouch.

What kind of bird am I?

A pelican

My head has no feathers, and I eat dead animals!

What kind of bird am I?

A vulture

Glossary

flamingo (fluh-MING-goh): A flamingo eats shrimp. This turns its feathers pink.

owl (OUL): An owl is a bird of prey—it hunts and eats other animals.

pelican (PEL-uh-kuhn): A pelican can hold up to 3 gallons (11 liters) of water in its pouch.

penguin (PENG-gwin): A penguin uses its wings as flippers to swim in the ocean.

vulture (VUHL-chur): Vultures are important—they clean up dead animals that could spread disease.

Index

What Is a Bird?
A bird is an animal with two legs, wings, feathers, and a beak. It is warm-blooded, which means its body temperature stays about the same. Female birds lay eggs.

School-to-Home Support for Caregivers and Teachers

This book helps children grow by letting them practice reading. Here are a few guiding questions to help the reader build his or her comprehension skills. Possible answers appear here in red.

Before Reading

- **What do I think this book is about?** I think this book is about different kinds of birds. I think this book is about the types of food that birds eat.
- **What do I want to learn about this topic?** I want to learn more about birds that can't fly. I want to learn more about owls.

During Reading

- **I wonder why...** I wonder why penguins have feathers but can't fly. I wonder why some birds eat dead animals.
- **What have I learned so far?** I have learned that owls have big, round eyes that can see at night. I have learned that flamingos eat shrimp that turns their feathers pink.

After Reading

- **What details did I learn about this topic?** I have learned that an owl is a bird of prey. I have learned that a pelican can hold up to 3 gallons (11 liters) of water in its pouch.
- **Read the book again and look for the glossary words.** I see the word *owl* on page 8, and the word *penguin* on page 13. The other glossary words are found on pages 22 and 23.

Library and Archives Canada Cataloguing in Publication

CIP available at Library and Archives Canada

Library of Congress Cataloging-in-Publication Data

CIP available at Library of Congress

Crabtree Publishing Company
www.crabtreebooks.com 1–800–387–7650

Written by: Taylor Farley
Print coordinator: Katherine Berti

Print book version produced jointly with Blue Door Education in 2023

Printed in the U.S.A./072022/CG20220201

PHOTO CREDITS:
Flamingo feathers © val lawless, flamingo birds © mexrix; owl at night © PAKULA PIOTR, Owl © Chris Hill; penguins © vladsilver; pelicans © Wang LiQiang; vulture head © Steve Meese, vulture © EcoPrint **All photos from www.Shutterstock.com**

Published in the United States
Crabtree Publishing
347 Fifth Ave.
Suite 1402-145
New York, NY 10016

Published in Canada
Crabtree Publishing
616 Welland Ave.
St. Catharines, Ontario
L2M 5V6